# Tiny H nds
## little feet

First Printing . . . . September 2008 . . . 2.5M

Second Printing . . October 2011 . . . . . 1M


© August 2008 Carlisle Press

ISBN 10 digit: 1-933-753-10-2

ISBN 13 digit: 978-1-933-753-10-2

*Cover and text design: Amy Diane Wengerd*

2673 Township Road 421
Sugarcreek, OH 44681
Carlisle Press  1.800.852.4482

# Table of Contents

# Framed Impressions

*Written in memory of the imprints that were made of
Naomi's hands and feet.*

The cracks and lines
on the bottoms of
feet and on the
palms of hands,
tell us that God specifically
designed Baby the
way He understands.

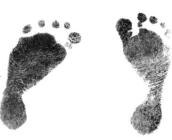

They are not just
impressions on paper,
Baby's tiny fists
can be curled.
Little feet can kick,
God knew who
He would pick.

Clay imprints
can be made,
the lines are
intricately carved,
with care.

Baby's pattern
is put in a
frame for
us to share.

-Kathy

# Mending Hope

*Written because I find healing and comfort in God's plan, when all
the pieces don't fit the way I think they should.*

There is a thread of hope,
Words can't mend,
But a stitch of love
Will repair the
Ache of a tear,
But the memories
Will always be there.

Different textures,
We are God's treasures,
Each piece has a story
Of value to lure,
Variety of shapes
And colors so pure.

God does the piecing,
He has a specific design
That won't be tattered,
When all else is shattered.

A gorgeous heirloom
So bold,
God's legacy is ours
To hold.

*-Kathy*

# *introduction*

I GREW UP IN A HOME OF SEVEN GIRLS AND FIVE boys. My dad was in the army from 1958-1978. My mom stayed at home to rear a lively batch of boys and seven inquisitive girls. Our house buzzed with an overactive bunch of children.

We moved from Germany to the United States when I was eight years old. My parents weren't reared in Christian homes, and I wasn't either. When we lived in Harrisburg, Oregon, my parents took us to a Baptist church. Our neighbors were Mennonites. I often played with their daughter. We had grand times of laughter and climbing their storage shed rafters. I also went to church with her. She invited me to school a couple of times. That was our first taste of how Mennonites lived.

Later we moved to Portland, Oregon. I missed my friend a lot, but we frequently wrote each other and kept the phone lines hot.

In the spring of 1989, our family (except Dad) went to the Porter Mennonite Church for the first time. Dad joined us a year later.

In the fall of 1992, I moved to Aroda, Virginia, where I started nurse's training. I graduated in the spring of 1994.

During nurse's training, I began dating Aaron Mast, who later became my husband. We were married in October 1994. We moved from Oregon to Kentucky in 1996, where we now reside.

We have two children who keep me busy as a mom. I desire another baby, but have surrendered those dreams to God.

I'm sitting in my dining room as the warm sunshine filters in through the dirty smudges that are on the windows. The steady flow of the sun's rays warms my soul.

I rely on God's help in writing my story. It is my desire that God will use my story to encourage and help other women who have lost a baby.

I bare my heart in these pages. Every time I write, my heart heals a little more, and I know I am doing something to honor God.

Tiny Hands

# the good news

I FELT EXCITED WHEN I DISCOVERED WE WOULD be blessed with a another baby. Aaron and I both felt God had answered our prayers after about eight years without being able to conceive. "Momma," my daughter Larissa said, "I wish we could have a little baby. Lyndall's little baby brother is so cute. I wish I could have a baby sister or brother too."

I had longings for a little one of my own too. Watching other mothers cradle their tiny babies stirred emotions in me. My mind pondered these thoughts. "Momma, did you hear me?" Larissa interrupted my thoughts.

I looked over at my daughter. "Yes, I heard you, and a baby would be nice. But just wishing doesn't bring one. You can pray for a baby, okay?"

"Okay," Larissa answered slowly.

My husband and I already knew God had answered our prayers. We knew the time would seem so long if we told our children too early, even though we could hardly wait to tell them the good news. I felt excited about a baby joining our family.

I went to the OB/GYN for the first time. He was ecstatic to hear about my pregnancy. I fell sick from May until August, fighting dehydration and nausea constantly. Every time I went in for an appointment I would ask, "Is it normal to be so sick all the time?"

The doctor would reply, "Yes, that is a sign of a healthy pregnancy." So I took his word for granted.

I was just emerging from three months of constant nausea and vomiting when we decided to tell our children about the baby. It was rewarding to see delight written all over their eager little faces. They would ask, "Momma, are we really going to have a baby?"

I responded with joy, "Yes, God has answered our prayers." They could hardly wait till I would wear a maternity dress, so they could tell their friends about the baby.

Sunday morning arrived all too soon. *I finally get to wear my new maternity dress!* Despite the morning sickness, I looked forward to letting others know.

At church that day, Aaron and I received many congratulations. As I glanced over at my husband receiving congratulations, his big grin thrilled my soul. His eyes sparkled with enthusiasm and joy.

A month later, Aaron being on a business trip, I went in to have an ultrasound. My appointment got canceled due to a delivery the doctor had to make. That week, my sister Amanda stayed with me while Aaron was gone.

As weeks passed, my anticipation to know and hold my baby grew. Aaron and I would pray for our baby, as we had done with our other two children. It was such a joyful time for our family to anticipate a little one. I had so many hopes and plans for this precious baby that was within me.

Then came the day of the ultrasound. It was a routine four-month exam to determine the heartbeat and measurements. After waiting for a half hour, the nurse finally called my name. I hopped up onto the examination table with delight just to be able to see our baby. The screen showed perfect little arms and tiny feet and a heart with a steady beat.

The nurse kept looking at the screen and moving the probe all over to determine the measurements of the baby's head. She said with a hint of reservation, "I can't get an accurate measurement because the baby won't hold still." The nurse left the room with a worried expression on her face. I began to feel a little apprehensive.

The doctor and the nurse came back into the room. Fear kept rising in my mind like a thick cloud of fog. Such stillness and dread as the doctor directed the probe over my belly, looking intently at the screen.

He kept looking at the baby's head. He began to take measurements, typing something into the computer, freezing the image and then letting it go again. Then more measurements and more typing.

Finally the doctor looked over at me. "Your baby's head is not normal. She has anencephaly." As I lay on the cold, hard examination table, fear was building a brick wall around my heart to keep out the pain. Unbidden tears trickled down my cheeks.

The silence left an eerie feeling in the air. Anguish flowed to the depth of my soul, and my heart cried out in such despair. Why? All my dreams to raise and watch my baby grow vanished before my eyes. I had tarried for this baby. I felt such an intense loss and emptiness. Why couldn't I keep her? I loved, wanted and carried her. I felt attached to her. Finally I asked the doctor, "What is anencephaly?"

He responded kindly, "It's when the top of the baby's head isn't closed. The baby's condition is fatal. It's called a neural tube defect."

The baby's hand came into view, and she stuck her thumb into her mouth. I asked, "How can a baby that has anencephaly be able to suck its thumb?"

The doctor replied, "In the womb, babies with anencephaly respond very much like a normal, healthy newborn."

Oh, the shock and pain of it all. No baby to cradle. I would go through all this pain and have nothing. I gathered my thoughts together. "Will the baby even cry or move?" I asked.

"No," the doctor replied.

I was so scared of giving birth to a baby that would hold completely still, a baby that wouldn't even cry.

I tried to process all the doctor was saying, but I felt in my heart that I needed time to face the reality of broken dreams and the why of it all.

I slowly scooted forward, and stepped off the examination

table. I thought the ceiling lights were going dim. The room started to spin. I felt cool and clammy. A tingling sensation went up and down my back.

The nurse hurriedly grabbed my elbow and said, "Kathy, are you okay? Your face is white."

I numbly shook my head as the tears slid down my cheeks.

The nurse led me through the door and down the hall to another room. *How did this happen and what now?* I kept asking myself. I felt all alone and forsaken from the verdict the doctor had just given me. It was almost like being in a courtroom and the doctor had just given me a death sentence.

I wiped my wet cheeks with the back of my hand. The nurse silently walked out of the room and softly closed the door. Click. I pondered, *Is this it?* I rummaged blindly through my purse searching for my cell phone. Finally my fingers touched the smooth, flat surface with tiny bumps. Managing to push in a phone number with shaky fingers, I tried to remain calm. I needed desperately to talk with someone.

The line connected. Ring. Ring. "Hello," Naomi said.

My voice quivering through tears and hiccups, I blurted out, "My baby isn't going to live."

"What do you mean, Kathy?" Naomi asked.

"My baby has no head." Another torrent of tears.

"Kathy, did you call Aaron?"

"I can't get a hold of him." I hiccupped again.

"I'll be praying for you, and keep trying to call Aaron."

"Okay," I answered.

I pushed the cell phone off. My friend hasn't experienced this kind of loss, and probably couldn't fully understand, but I needed her shoulder to cry on.

The nurse knocked on the door. Tap. Tap. I heard the door-knob turn. Squeak. The nurse softly entered the room. She slipped me a white tissue. I wiped my dripping nose.

As if in a fog, I heard the doctor say from the hallway, "I am going to send you for a second opinion." The nurse made the appointment and gave me the card. I slowly exited through the door. Click. The door swung shut. As I scanned across the waiting room at all the pregnant women, I wished it weren't me. *Why couldn't this cup pass from me?* I kept pondering these thoughts as I left through the door to go outside.

I retrieved my cell phone from my purse and tried Aaron again. Ring. Ring. The lines connected. Through tears I said, "Aaron, our baby isn't going to live."

"Kathy, calm down. Tell me what is wrong."

I tried desperately to quit crying. Finally I said, "Aaron, please come and get me."

"Allright." Aaron hung up.

Aaron immediately left work to join me. When he arrived, I let the tears fall uncontrollably as he held me with a warm, protective embrace. The dream of the baby we had held in our hearts vanished before our eyes.

I felt robbed. Nothing else seemed to matter. *Why me? This can't be real.* I wanted my baby so very much. I longed for a baby to cuddle and hold. My world seemed like it had ended. My hopes, dreams and expectations were gone.

# Tiny Hands
## *are there answers?*

WHAT IS ANENCEPHALY?[1] I WONDERED. I scanned my memory for every detail I had heard about the condition in nurse's training and pored over medical texts and articles. Some of the most helpful information I found was presented by the National Institute of Health in Bethesda, Maryland, describing how anencephaly is a defect in the closure of the neural tube during fetal development. The neural tube is a narrow channel that folds and closes between the third and fourth weeks of pregnancy to form the brain and spinal cord of the embryo. Anencephaly occurs when the "cephalic" or head end of the neural tube fails to close, resulting in the absence of a major portion of the brain, skull and scalp. Infants with this disorder are born without a forebrain (the front part of the brain) and a cerebrum (the thinking and coordinating part of the brain). The remaining brain tissue is often exposed—not covered by bone or skin. A baby

*[1]see diagram on page* 71

born with anencephaly is usually blind, deaf, unconscious and unable to feel pain. Although some individuals may be born with a rudimentary brain stem, the lack of a functioning cerebrum permanently rules out the possibility of ever gaining consciousness. Reflex actions such as breathing and responses to sound or touch may occur.

The cause of anencephaly is unknown. Although it is thought that a mother's diet and vitamin intake may play a role, doctors believe that many factors are involved.

Is there any treatment? There is no cure or standard treatment for anencephaly.

What is the prognosis? The prognosis for babies with anencephaly is extremely poor. If the infant is not stillborn, then he or she will usually die within a few hours or days after birth.

I wanted to isolate myself from everyone because someone would surely bring attention to my pregnancy.

My pregnancy was supposed to be a happy occasion. It wasn't. My pregnancy became a heavy burden. Every time I felt my baby move I felt such extreme sorrow. Every kick reminded me of her precious life, and yet she was to die. I would never know her as I knew my other two children. These thoughts broke my heart. I felt like I had lost part of myself.

I wanted to hibernate until my pregnancy was over. I didn't really want to deal with it. I struggled when I saw other pregnant women.

The day of the 3-D ultrasound arrived. My in-laws went with Aaron and me to Evansville, Indiana, for the second opinion.

While we were waiting in the luxurious office of the OB specialist, I still hung onto my last thread of hope. Could my regular OB doctor be wrong about the diagnosis?

The nurse called my name. She directed us to a room with a 3-D ultrasound machine sitting at one end. The machine loomed up at me with a foreboding tale to tell. I stepped up onto the hard, cold table with apprehension.

I wanted to see my baby on the ultrasound screen, knowing this might be the last time I get to see her alive. Part of me was in denial. I just couldn't understand and accept the severity of the situation. My heart knew how bad it was, but I felt so sure God would heal my baby. I pleaded with God to let me keep my little one.

The nurse took the pictures, and then got up to leave the room with a sympathetic look on her face. She returned with a genetic specialist. As he greeted my husband and me, his eyes met ours with genuine concern. After looking at the pictures, he said, "Your baby's condition is fatal."

Tears streamed down my cheeks as I realized that my last thread of hope had been snatched from my grasp.

The specialist stated in a kind voice, "I want to discuss with you some more about your baby down in my office." He got up to leave the room.

The room wanted to spin in circles as I got down from the examination table. As I was putting on my dress, I felt powerless as to what I could do to stop this nightmare. My thoughts were racing. *What can I do to stop this? How can I*

*make my baby healthy? Why do I have to go through this?* I
longed for my baby.

Aaron said, "Kathy, come on. You can't just block out reality." I tried desperately to focus my mind. My pain-filled eyes
met his. I couldn't reply.

Aaron guided me out the door. As we approached the
specialist's office, everything looked dark and gloomy to me.
I wanted to run down the hall, away from it all, but I knew
that wasn't a possibility.

The specialist invited us in and asked us to have a seat. As
we sat down on the plush couch, he walked across the room
to his overstuffed, plaid chair.

He cleared his throat and slowly began, "I am truly sorry. I
can feel for you, because my wife and I lost a daughter with
a heart defect." His eyes were misty with tears of sympathy.
"There will be no medical measures done on your baby to
prolong life."

I tried to focus on what he was saying. It broke my heart
to try to comprehend, yet he was very kind as he shared the
prognosis.

As we got up to leave, Aaron checked out, and I walked
through the door, wanting to never go back. My tears came
faster now as I approached my in-laws. My mother-in-law
followed me out the door. We walked down the hall to ride
the elevator to the main floor. I wanted to walk where no one
could see me, but decided that wasn't logical. I went straight
to the van. Aaron and his dad arrived at the van, and we drove
home in silence.

Our children were at their grandparents' house when we arrived home. Aaron and I knew we had to tell the children about the baby. Two days later, we finally told them the news. They were so disappointed when we told them that the baby wasn't going to live. Oh, our hearts ached with them as their chins began to quiver and the tears started to flow down their soft cheeks. My mother heart knew how badly they wanted to keep their sister.

At a time of deep hurt, we have our choices to make, I have often heard. I knew we could let the circumstances make us better or bitter. Yet my heart was too numb to grasp that truth.

The days after learning about the diagnosis of the baby were agonizing and stressful. A Scripture verse kept coming to my mind. "The eyes of the Lord are upon the righteous, and his ears are open unto their cry." (Psalm 34:15).

*Why isn't God hearing my heart's cry?* I often wondered. I wanted God to heal my precious baby. I knew He could, but it wasn't His will at that time. There is a reason that God chose me to carry this special child. Maybe He wanted me to be able to someday help someone else.

Oh, all the sorrow and grief I went through at the time of learning that our baby had anencephaly. Truly, Heaven will be worth every heartache. We may not know the reason why now, but in Heaven we will. God really does care. Through this experience, I have drawn closer to Him.

In November, three months before my February 18, 2005, due date, I had an urge to write a poem. I never realized we'd be using it two weeks later.

# the beginning of the end

I BEGAN GETTING SICK, AND MY STOMACH WAS hard as a rock. I called the OB doctor and told him what was happening. He asked me to come to his office immediately. I called Aaron at work and told him what the doctor had said. He left work right away and joined me in the waiting room. When the nurse called my name, I followed Aaron back to an exam room.

The doctor came in hurriedly and ordered an ultrasound. He looked at the pictures closely and, looking my husband in the eye, said, "Either terminate the pregnancy or lose both of them. Kathy's fluid is building up quickly."

We wanted to wait, but it wasn't what God had intended for us. My husband wheeled me back to the operating room. As I was coasting down the cold hallway on two wheels, tears were flowing uncontrollably down my cheeks. I wasn't ready to deliver my baby, because I kept her safe within my womb.

I loved her with such a fervent love. I had carried her and provided a warm and secure environment for her for seven months. She acted like a normal baby. She would kick and wiggle.

Reality was, though, that she was going to be born on December 3, 2004. My thoughts were in a whirl. *Why can't I keep her? See, she's moving!* The last time I felt her move within me was after I climbed up onto the cold, hard operating table.

Such despair and fear kept wrapping their little strands of thread around my heart and mind. I couldn't see my husband anywhere in the room. My eyes were searching the room for him.

Finally the doctor's eyes met mine with compassion. He took my hand as I went to sleep. Several hours later I woke up in a bright room. I felt drowsy. As soon as the nurse had my pain bearable, in came the visitors. I can't recall most of them. I thought I kept seeing my sister-in-law with the visitors, but Aaron told me later, "No, she wasn't there." My mind was groggy from all the pain medication.

My mom had made a soft white blanket with a rose embroidered onto it. I held the blanket in my hands and brought it to my face. It was soft and warm and cuddly. Naomi was wrapped in this blanket when I first held her.

From the other side of the room a bright flash caught my attention and I looked up. There, with a camera, stood my mom taking pictures. Her eyes were red and swollen, but she smiled anyway.

I didn't want to hold my little girl at first. *How am I going to cope with looking at her for the first time?* I wondered.

The minute she was laid in my arms my fears vanished. Naomi Jewel was precious, rare and gorgeous. She was my beautiful little girl, uniquely formed and given to me from God. Instantly, more love filled my heart, and I knew that I didn't want to let her go.

I was able to cradle my baby, with help. I noticed she had tiny features. She reminded me of our other daughter, but she had our son's nose. I held her close to my breast and wanted desperately for her to be normal, so I could keep her. She made no sound. I gazed into her tiny eyes which held a momentary sparkle. Then, like an extinguished flame, the sparkle vanished. *Can you see me?* I wanted to scream. *Do you know that I'm your momma?* But I knew it was futile. I held her little hand as she grasped my finger ever so slightly. The feeling was grand, but her eyes finally fluttered to a close. She lived two hours and thirty-nine minutes.

I treasured the opportunity to hold Naomi in my arms as I lovingly held her little, warm, soft hand. But then I had to say good-bye. Holding Naomi was the most joyous moment in my life, even amidst all the pain I felt. I will always be thankful that I at least had that opportunity. My Naomi Jewel was a gem, precious and rare. She slipped away to be with Jesus. It was a bittersweet moment.

I was relieved to know that I could have a room in a different section of the hospital. I didn't want to hear anyone's baby crying. The doctor provided my husband and me a safe haven within the hospital so we could be with our child. He made sure we weren't disturbed. It was a place where I could hold and love my baby. My husband and children were also able to hold her, rock her, kiss her and spend time examining her tiny features.

The nurse had wrapped Naomi Jewel in a blanket and brought her to Aaron while I was still in the recovery room. I had no idea how much time had slipped by when I finally awoke. Time was meaningless for me. Aaron brought Naomi Jewel over to me. I held Naomi's tiny, still body and looked at her. I thought how Naomi would never cry, never nurse and never smile at me.

Every time I heard someone ask about Naomi, I cringed inside, thinking that this was just a bad dream. Soon family and friends left, and a nurse came and took Naomi for some pictures.

When the nurse returned with Naomi, she was dressed in a white gown and cap and wrapped in a soft white blanket. The nurse also gave us a red artificial rose, and a poem with her little footprints on it.

Giving Naomi Jewel over to the nurse to be taken to the morgue was the hardest thing I ever had to do. It's been over two and a half years now as I write this, but I can barely see the page as the tears spill and blot my writing. I still yearn to go back and just hold her once again. I can hardly imagine the thought of my tiny baby girl lying in the cold basement of the hospital morgue. It sounded cruel.

*Lord, you knew all along the pain I was going to have to*

*bear.* I lay on the hospital bed silent and still. *Why me?* my thoughts kept asking. *Why did this have to happen? Don't you love me anymore? Why take my baby?*

Suddenly the lab technician flipped on the light, saying, "It's time to draw your blood."

*Ugh,* I groaned inwardly. *What time is it? It's still dark outside. This is going to hurt again.*

The technician walked briskly over to my bed, and said, "Stick out your arm."

I said groggily through half-closed eyelids, "I feel like a pincushion."

The lab technician's mouth turned upward in a huge grin. She looked into my eyes and said, "Kathy, I know it hurts, but we have to draw the blood to determine how many red blood cells you have."

Stunned, I looked at Aaron with fear in my eyes. Finally I got the courage to ask, "What do you mean?"

The lab technician's eyes held mine for a minute. She softly said, "The doctor has ordered a red blood count. You'll have to ask the nurse for further details." The lab technician put her blood supplies away and walked across the room. She opened the door. Click. "Good-bye," she said, waving.

Questions kept popping into my mind left and right. *Why the blood? What is going on?* Panic hit me, and I started to weep uncontrollably. I buried my face in the white sheet. I wanted to block out the pain of my heart. I wanted to block out the hurt.

*No! No!* My thoughts kept hurdling over and over. *This*

*can't be real. I just lost a baby and now this.* It seemed a burden too heavy to bear at that moment. I experienced sheer grief and terror.

Minutes ticked by slowly. Minutes turned into hours. I knew the inevitable was yet to come, but when? Dawn hadn't made its way across the horizon yet as I drifted into a slumber.

Knock, knock. I faintly heard a soft knocking sound at the door. I turned over in the bed and sat up sleepily. In walked the doctor, wearing white garb.

Suddenly fear entered again. I felt my eyes bulging out of their sockets.

My doctor looked kindly at me. He said, "Kathy, the nurse has informed me you have questions about the lab work I ordered. The reason I ordered the lab work is because you lost too much blood during surgery and your uterus was on the verge of erupting. I couldn't tell what was blood or fluid. Your lab results are reading that you need at least three to four units of blood. You will be all right after the required amount of blood has gotten into your body."

The doctor's words rang like bells over and over in my mind.

The doctor patted my shoulder and reassured me that everything would be all right. He got up, and walked softly over to the door. He reached for the doorknob and turned it. Squeak. He turned around. "I will see you later this evening."

Aaron and I started talking at once, interrupting each other. Questions flew unanswered. Suddenly I felt incredibly weak and tired. I slumped back onto the pillow and lay there, wanting to be left alone.

Aaron picked up the phone from the cradle and dialed. He talked to his mom about what the doctor had informed us.

My nurse entered the room. "Kathy, you need to consider taking the blood this morning."

I looked at my nurse and said, "I would like to get blood from my family."

She responded, "I'm sorry, but that process will take too long. You need the blood as soon as possible."

"Okay."

I had no idea what this would all be like. All I wanted was to be free of physical and emotional pain. I was so weak I could hardly sit up in bed. Recovery was long. In time I did get stronger. Some days it was difficult to function because my emotions were going up and down. I felt like I existed from one moment to the next. I thought I couldn't go on, yet I did survive day by day with God carrying me in His arms.

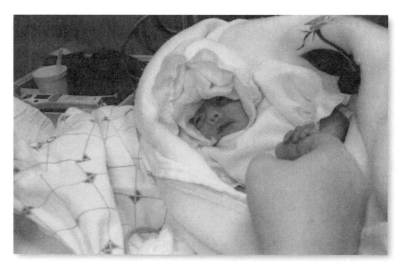

Holding Naomi's finger, while she grasps mine ever
so slightly, just moments before she died.

Aaron and Kathy Mast with children,
Jaron, Michael, Josiah and Larissa.

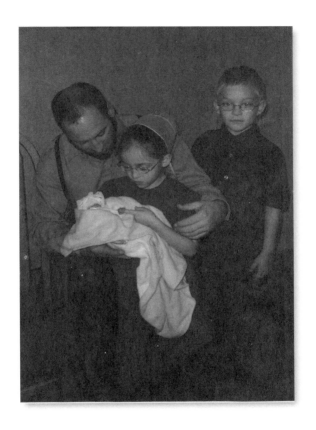

My husband Aaron and our children Jaron and Larissa
share precious moments holding Naomi Jewel.

Holding little Naomi Jewel, is a friend Naomi
Cross for whom Naomi Jewel was named.

# Tiny Hands *carried through*

GOD BLESSED US WITH TWO HOURS AND thirty-nine minutes of her life here on earth. We thought she wasn't going to live at all. Naomi Jewel met and touched the lives of our family and friends. Our journey with Naomi Jewel was not always easy, but it was our time to love and cherish her.

Numerous people from the church and Aaron's workplace came to the hospital to give their condolences. My family put the poem I had written on a doily, along with a picture of my hand holding little Naomi's. The nurses commented on how the poem encouraged them. They also said, "We have never seen so many people come to this hospital before to see one person."

As we left the hospital, my mind was groggy and numb. We were to go home to get dressed for the burial. Everyone was running to and fro as we entered the house. Then silence filled the air, because everyone stopped and just looked as I came through the door. Such stillness was only for a moment until they realized that I was still part of the family. I stared blankly at my children. Their eyes mirrored my own grief. I was reminded that I'm not the only one mourning.

The weather was cold, breezy, cloudy and wet for December. The hilltop where we sat to watch people bury Naomi seemed rather bleak.

As we were driving to our baby's funeral, I kept hearing a song being played. The van pulled up to the grave site and the engine stopped. The door was swung open, and Aaron helped me down. We sat on cold, metal chairs provided for us, with family and friends standing behind us. I was shivering from the cold, and felt someone put a blanket around my shoulders. I felt a sense of protection due to that person.

Oh, how I wanted to scream, *Please let me keep my baby. Don't bury her. What did I do to deserve such a blow to my heart?*

With all the pain I endured, I kept trying to stay seated without falling off the chair. Aaron was crying beside me. *Why can't I cry?* The tears wouldn't come. I blocked out the whole burial service. I was mourning deeply; my tears could be seen by God, but not by man. I cried within my heart, *My Naomi is gone. She really is dead!* I wince and cringe at the memories. I heard only one thing during the service—our minister reading my poem.

I couldn't stand to hear the scraping of the dirt and stones as they fell onto Naomi's white casket. Each shovelful was like a physical blow to my heart. I kept thinking, *You are putting dirt on my baby. Please stop.*

I knew we would never be the same complete family, because Naomi was gone. The circle would always be broken.

After the service, we drove back up the hill toward home. Again I heard the song being played. Later I discovered the song I heard on a tape was "Walk in Love." The song talked about forgiveness when you have been forsaken. The words meant a lot to me.

My husband and children hurt too. It was difficult to see the pain in their eyes. It seemed the spark of joy was gone. I wasn't the only one who would miss our little bundle to cuddle.

Aaron felt drained. He wanted to be strong through this whole ordeal. Sometimes he pretended he was just fine, but on the inside he hurt deeply. I read the sadness in his eyes. I expected him to feel or behave exactly the way I felt. I realized that wasn't the answer to the problem. Aaron needed to grieve in his own way.

Our relationship grew and became stronger through this experience. We stayed focused on God. He carried us through this difficult time. When I finally discussed with Aaron how much I miss my baby, he opened up. He felt the same way. We would talk and share our hearts together.

One morning as I was having my devotions, I found these Scripture verses. They meant a lot to me. "He healeth the broken in heart, and bindeth up their wounds. He telleth the number of the stars; he calleth them all by their names. Great is our Lord, and of great power: his understanding is infinite" (Psalm 147:3-5).

My heart began the road to healing. I struggled at first because I didn't want to take the first step. Finally I took the first step by telling God my hurt.

I read and reread different portions of the Psalms. Verses from Psalm 147 really stood out the most to me, and became a balm to soothe my hurt. God put an ointment on my broken and wounded heart by allowing me to talk about my feelings to a dear friend.

It is important to express your feelings and allow yourself to grieve. I had a close friend to whom I could talk. She sat and listened and cried with me. I felt like I was riding a roller coaster at times with my feelings. *I'm in a valley and can't get out. Where do I go from here?* I kept pondering. It takes a lot of work to climb up a mountain, but with God ALL things are possible. He held my hand as we climbed up the mountain of grief. My healing didn't come quickly. It was a process I needed to work through with time.

God knew the name of our baby and her condition before we did. "Before I formed thee in the belly I knew thee" (Jeremiah 1:5a). He called Naomi Jewel home by her name. What a comforting thought!

My burden became lighter. I began to have a peace that God was holding my hand during this difficult time. God gave me the strength I needed to go on. "I will never leave thee, nor forsake thee" (Hebrews 13:5b). I am thankful that God never left me nor forsook me.

In six weeks or so, I felt like I was getting back to normal. Emotionally I was still unsteady, and not prepared for what lay ahead.

One Sunday our little girl came home from church very distressed. She said angrily, "Momma, if Naomi had lived, she would be just like \_\_\_\_\_'s baby. It's not fair that they get to keep their baby and we don't."

"Naomi Jewel is in a better place," we told her. "We loved her just like you, but God wants her to fill a special place in Heaven."

We had told our children how Naomi wasn't going to live. Our tears mingled as we cried together. They were sad over the loss of their little sister. Both children asked numerous questions such as, "Did Naomi go to Heaven?" "Why did she have to die?" and "Why couldn't we keep her?" We answered their questions honestly. We explained to them that death is a part of life. Yes, Naomi is in Heaven with Jesus.

Both children expressed a fear of, "Will Momma die too?" We explained to them, "No, not now!" We showed them ways that God loves and cares for them. We held them as they cried.

When Naomi was born the children held their precious little sister. Oh, what sadness radiated from their eyes!

We read a story together as a family. The name of the book

was *In Memory of Michael* by Wanda M. Yoder. The book really encouraged and helped our children get an understanding of death, and how others face death too. Our children slowly came to the place of accepting Naomi's death.

In learning from others, I concluded that they all cared and prayed for us. As the fog lifted, I saw light at the end of the tunnel. I knew God was on the throne. Once again my heart was at peace.

Even with time I kept asking, "Why, God? Why me? What do you want to teach me?" My loss was great, but God guided me every step of the way. He held my hand.

My mind still can't grasp all the memories. My arms ached to hold my baby. The grief overwhelmed my senses.

A book called *Free to Grieve* helped me to realize that these patterns of grieving were normal, and that it takes time to heal.

Writing my story and poems brought a healing balm to my aching heart and empty arms. I shed many a tear over our loss, but really, we didn't lose. Naomi is in Heaven where she is perfect, and I can see her again someday—if I am faithful to God and His Word.

Naomi is our daughter forever. She is healthy and pure in Heaven.

There is a quote that I like: "Children are the hands by which we take hold of Heaven." This quote is comforting to me as it makes Heaven a little closer to our hearts.

Throughout the dark storm of grief, I knew that God was

my anchor and my rock.

Gradually I began to think of Naomi's death with a trusting acceptance. God's plan never fails. I began to see that my happiness is not based on circumstances. God's joy flows in my heart from reading the Bible and talking with friends and family.

Our Naomi draws Heaven a little closer to us. We are able to empathize with others who have lost a precious baby. God has drawn our family closer together through this experience.

## new beginnings

AS SPRING APPROACHED, SO DID MY yearning to do something. I began to prepare my garden and flower beds for planting. Preparing the soil was a task. I got out the tiller after my husband disked and plowed the garden for me.

The garden and flowers I planted were good therapy for me. It took my mind off myself and helped me to focus on something that would benefit my family and neighbors. It took long, tiring days to get my garden ready to plant. The garden became a hiding place for me. When down on my knees planting and digging through the soil, the garden became my refuge—a place I could go and release pent-up energy. It gave me something to do instead of giving up. As soil slipped through my fingers, I concentrated on how God worked in my life. Oftentimes I wet the soil with my tears when I thought about my baby. I would again refocus on asking God to help me through these lonely times of the day. As the sun shone brightly in the sky, so did God's love for me.

New life was taking place in my heart as well as in the soil in which I planted seeds. My garden and flower beds, as they bloomed, reminded me of how God can work miracles. I am really fond of roses. As their blooms opened up, the petals took on such glorious beauty. They were refreshing and cheerful to my heart. The roses brought comfort to me, because God's love has never failed. He helped me to concentrate on my garden and roses, so that I wouldn't get lonely and think just of myself. "Thou art my hiding place; thou shalt preserve me from trouble; thou shalt compass me about with songs of deliverance" (Psalm 32:7).

As the fragrance of the roses filled the air, so the arms of God surrounded me with His love and comfort. It flowed through me and around me.

One day, preparing to plant flowers in my hanging baskets on the porch, I found a wren nest. It looked about the size of a teacup. It is among the most delicate treasures I have found this spring. When I saw the fragility of the teacup-sized nest that held the jelly bean-sized eggs, I felt just as exposed and vulnerable from the grief that was in my heart. And yet, God designed the bird's dwelling to withstand any damage the weather would cause and He would protect its precious contents.

My heart and yours can weather the storms of life with God's help. As we allow God to comfort and carry us through, we will discover once again that our hearts will have peace.

As the weeks went by, our children and I kept a close watch on the eggs. One morning I lifted the hanging basket off its hook and looked inside. To my delight, the eggs were finally hatched. The children clapped their hands gleefully. As I watched their enthusiasm and excitement over their discovery, the joy that radiated from their chubby little faces showed me that as the tiny eggs hatched out into something great and full of life, God was showing out of His love that through grief can come something precious and beautiful.

The wrens fed their babies, and they grew bigger and bigger. They would make a peep, peep sound as the adults fed them. We were able to see them stick their heads above the nest with their mouths wide open as they received food. Finally we didn't hear any more peep, peep sounds coming through the open screen door from the nest.

God took care of me during my deepest hurt. He lovingly nurtured and fed me daily. I read His Word and prayed often. As I struggled through the raging storms of grief, I looked to God for the strength I needed to hold on till I found rest.

There were days when I had to continually kneel before God, telling Him over and over how I felt inside. I wanted to bar the doors of my heart from everything. No matter how we feel inside, we do not have to be ashamed to turn to God. "Hear my prayer, O Lord, and let my cry come unto thee. Hide not thy face from me in the day when I am in trouble" (Psalm 102:1-2). These verses were a healing balm to my aching heart. I poured out my heart to God while the tears flowed down my cheeks.

When we feel lonely, let's look to God. We have the freedom to tell Him everything that is in our most secret chambers. God won't turn you away. He will always be there.

My heart is broken, yet mending. My baby enriched my life. She brought me more love for others, she brought Heaven closer, and she brought appreciation for all that have supported me through my loss.

"To everything there is a season, and a time to every purpose under heaven. A time to be born, and a time to die; a time to plant, and a time to pluck up that which is planted... A time to weep, and a time to laugh; a time to mourn, and a time to dance" (Ecclesiastes 3:1, 2, 4). I have learned through these verses to accept and appreciate God's perfect timing. My tears were a healing element for overcoming all the ache that was stored up in the bins of my heart.

The Lord makes known His plans for us in unexpected ways. One of the blessings that has come from my grief is that I can be sensitive to others while they go through the loss of a baby. With God's direction for my life I want to be able to do this. There are no easy answers to the questions that are asked. But God's precious Word encourages us.

"My brethren, count it all joy when ye fall into divers temptations; knowing this, that the trying of your faith worketh patience. But let patience have her perfect work, that ye may be perfect and entire, wanting nothing" (James 1:2-4).

I needed to grow in steadfastness. I wasn't willing to endure all the pain with patience. God has helped me through this opportunity to lean on Him more in accepting the passing of

Naomi. Patience was something I wanted, but I couldn't grasp it by myself. I tried hard to have patience with my loss, but I couldn't do it alone. Only God can help us. He has helped me grow in this particular area. It took time, prayer, Bible reading and talking to a special friend. My friend helped me see that I needed to daily commit myself to telling God everything when it hurt so badly. Patience does not come automatically. It takes hard work. The process was slow. We must put effort into the process of producing patience.

I am thankful for a heart that has been broken. I'm also thankful that the death of Naomi has left me with a deeper and softer understanding towards the hurts of others.

# Tiny Hands

## *from fear to faith*

I DIDN'T REALIZE AT THE TIME THAT GOD would use my grief over our precious Naomi to draw me closer to Him and to help me be there for other women who grieve. I didn't know what the future held for me.

After I wrote the first part of my story (*Keepers at Home* Fall 2006), little did I realize that God would bless me with another baby.

Fear? Was I afraid of the uncertainty of another pregnancy? Was I afraid it would end like the last one? I was deathly scared. I was sure I would have another baby without a forehead.

My husband Aaron would tell me, "Trust in God. He will be with us."

The dictionary explains fear as an unpleasant, often strong, emotion caused by the anticipation of danger.

I faced such fear that when we pulled into the parking lot of the doctor's office, I grabbed my husband's hand as one who grabs for life, giving him a desperate look. I renewed the clutch and looked at him with fearful eyes, asking, "What am I to expect?"

What causes fear? Unusual things we do not understand can cause fear. Facing the unknown causes fear. I faced an unknown *what if*?

I have learned that fear is a lack of faith and trust in God. When we do not put our focus on God, fear arises. I faced fear throughout my whole pregnancy.

"Peace I leave with you, my peace I give unto you: not as the world giveth, give I unto you. Let not your heart be troubled, neither let it be afraid" (John 14:27).

I had a hard time dealing with the voice in my head that kept whispering, *What if? What if at the end of a long pregnancy this baby won't be normal?* I simply couldn't fathom a healthy baby. I prayed about my dilemma. I voiced my thoughts to a dear friend. My heart desperately longed for a normal, healthy newborn.

I had to hush my thoughts as best as I could... hoping, praying and waiting that all would be well.

Healing comes from God. His touch on those tender, raw places is a miracle. It doesn't come all at once. I look back now and don't feel the hurt the way I used to. God healed my wounded and crushed spirit. He covered me with His hands.

My thoughts wandered. *Will God allow this baby to be healthy?* I was terrified of another loss.

Yes, I knew God was in control. He wanted me to put my faith and trust completely in Him.

I tried to hide my questions and fears by stuffing them deep into my heart. Whenever something is hard to bear, I put up a wall around my heart so nothing can hurt me. I feel safe behind my wall. Hidden away in my heart I feel protected for a moment. I don't have to feel pain or loss in this secret place. It's a place to hide. But I can't always live outside reality. I finally ascended to face my problem. It's a problem of fear. God will help me face the truth. I feel safe in His presence. He is the one I am learning to run to for shelter. He sees all my pain and worries.

The first summer after Naomi's death I spent a lot of time in my strawberry patch and garden. I poured my energy into maintaining a weed-free garden.

One bright, humid, sunny morning as I stepped out the back door my son asked, "Momma, why do you look so sad today?" His question startled me. *I feel sad,* I thought. *But why? Can he really see the pain and silent cries of my heart?*

"Yes, Jaron, I am sad," I responded.

"How come?"

As I trudged out to the strawberry patch I kept pondering Jaron's question. "Are you still sad over Naomi dying?" Jaron finally asked once again.

*Lord, can Jaron really see my emotions? Does my son know how I miss Naomi? What is it like for her to be in God's presence and have no suffering?* Suddenly I realized Jaron was staring at me.

"Well, Jaron, I am sad that Naomi passed away, but I am also happy that she is in Heaven," I answered slowly. I could tell by Jaron's silence that he was pondering my words as he pulled thick green weeds from the dark, rich soil.

It's amazing how God works through children to show us how we reveal ourselves to them.

Meanwhile, Larissa was growing tired of pulling weeds. Several moments passed before I heard, "Here's a red, juicy strawberry!" Larissa brushed brown, wet leaves aside.

"I see only orange ones with a little green," Jaron said softly.

"Well, since I'm the only girl and found this one, I get to eat it!" Larissa exclaimed happily.

I gazed over at the children. All of a sudden, hop, hop. Jaron leaped over the strawberry rows and positioned his hands on his hips and said, "No, you're not! Naomi was a girl too."

Larissa stood up and studied Jaron over the top of her glasses. She shook her finger at him. "Naomi died, and she is not here to be considered a girl."

I was leaning over the strawberry row listening intently to their chatter. "O-oh," I groaned as I stood up. My eyes were misty from tears threatening to spill. Their argument died away. Softly I said, "Children, let's not argue. God had a different plan for Naomi's life. Yes, she was a girl and your sister."

The children looked at me with soft, sad eyes. Taking the hoe I shoved it into the soft dirt. *What are the children going to be asking next?*

The morning crept by slowly without more confrontations.

Several months later Jaron, Larissa and I flew out to Oregon to visit my family. While there I spent time with my sister Teresa, who held a foster baby. "Do you want to hold him?" she asked. For a long moment I tried desperately to flee the spot where I sat on the couch, but I couldn't budge. Everyone was still chattering away, but I wasn't paying attention.

Teresa spoke louder. "Kathy, did you hear what I said?"

My attention was drawn back to the present. I nodded my head. I felt overwhelmed at the possibility of holding a baby. Why? My thoughts were bobbing up and down like a sailboat blown around by a roaring windstorm. *This is going to be hard because I haven't held a baby since Naomi died. Will the raw, tender places be split open again? I sure hope not.* I silently prayed, *Lord, help me through this.*

The baby was a little four-month-old boy who had had an abused life. When my sister made the offer, I couldn't reach out my arms and accept the baby. I felt paralyzed. Teresa placed the baby on my lap and told me frankly, "Here, you need to hold him. It will be good for you."

I looked down into the little eyes that longed for trust and love. He didn't smile. His eyes held no warmth like a baby should. He just lay there in my arms, looking forlorn. I couldn't take my eyes off him. He felt so small and cuddly in my arms. That moment a poultice was being placed on my wounded sore. His tiny, blond eyebrows would rise in astonishment when I tried to get him to smile. My heart was heavy from knowing what had happened to him. It made it easier to hold and love him.

I called Aaron at work and told him, "I held a baby, and I enjoyed myself." I gazed at the tiny fingers and his sweet little face while talking with Aaron on the phone.

Aaron asked, "How did you hold the baby?"

I responded, "I couldn't do it by myself. Teresa helped me hold the baby." God can heal those wounded spots in our hearts. He understands our broken hearts, and He can free us from bondage. We can't see the whole picture like God can.

## new life

WEEKS PASSED AND I WAS LOOKING forward to becoming a mother once again. When I discovered I was pregnant, I knew God had answered my prayers.

We had an encounter with a family from Tennessee. We met them in Nashville at Vanderbilt Children's Hospital. Their baby girl was slowly losing her fight for life. She was so small and fragile when I saw her for the first time. As I walked through the door of the hospital room, I felt an urgency to run. Why? I felt trapped by my own loss. I silently prayed, *God, help me to be what you want me to be.* I couldn't quite imagine what lay ahead.

God wanted me to give encouragement. How we choose to relate our loss to others is very personal. It touches a spot deep within our soul. Helping others through their grief builds friendships. I have met many new friends. God brought Monika across my path so I could encourage her.

As I sat down in the wooden rocking chair, I gazed at Monika. She was talking rapidly and quietly. I didn't say much. I finally told Monika my story. I handed her a card along with the poem I had written during my own pain.

Four weeks later we received the news that Monika's little Jolene had passed away. Aaron and I drove to Tennessee to give our condolences to the dear family. As we were going through the line to shake hands, my thoughts were racing. *Here is a friend who understands my joy, my sorrow and my journey through grief.*

As I approached Monika, I clasped her cold hands in mine. I listened to her mother heart. I understood her sorrow! God brought Monika into my life at a time in my journey when I needed someone to relate to who understood my mother heart. Connecting with Monika provided healing.

Monika asked, "Is it okay that I used your poem for our obituary?"

I was startled for a moment, then I gathered my thoughts and replied, "Yes!"

Monika said, "I can't write poems, and the one you wrote fits my daughter."

How exciting to hear that God was using my poem to fit Monika's needs.

Larissa and Jaron were praying for another baby. They could hardly wait for their prayers to be answered.

"Hey, Momma!" shouted Larissa.

All I could hear was the humming of the rototiller. I was guiding it down between the rows of potatoes. Suddenly the rototiller sputtered to a stop. *Just great,* I thought to myself.

"Jaron, can you get Momma the red gas can?" I asked, huffing and puffing. Jaron ran off to get the gas can.

Meanwhile, Larissa called again, "Momma, look!"

I turned my head toward the sound of her voice. Larissa was running at full speed toward me with a handful of bright irises.

"Aren't these pretty, Momma?" asked Larissa.

"Yes, they are," I said.

Larissa continued, "Momma, can I have a garden of my own to plant my bulbs in? Charity has her own."

"No, not this year." I replied. "Can you wait until next year?"

Larissa looked up at me with such sad eyes. "I guess," came her quiet reply.

Larissa looked disappointed. She turned around and said, "Momma, I've been praying for a baby as long as I can remember, but my prayer hasn't been answered."

I looked up at her while plucking brown stems from the potato plants. "Larissa, God doesn't always give us what we want."

"Why not? My baby sister is dead. Dead!" said Larissa. Her voice rose an octave.

My heart was torn open once again. *When will the questioning end?*

With my heart hurting and my mind racing, I took Larissa into my arms and held her. I tasted salty tears as they slid down my cheeks. "Larissa, I know you hurt deep down in your heart, but you can't be angry. Momma hurts too. I miss Naomi like you do."

Larissa gazed up at me with tears flowing down her soft cheeks. "Momma, I love you." She picked up her bright, colorful blooms with her dirty, smudged hands and took off running. "I'll put these in a vase."

I experienced these same questions over and over from the children all summer long.

Two months later we joyfully announced to the children that a baby would be born sometime the following year. I felt an urgency of fear. *What's going to happen? Will I get the privilege of having a baby or not?* My thoughts were on a roller coaster ride, up and down and around. Finally I prayed, *Lord, be with me.*

My doctor's voice was the last thing I heard before the anesthesia put me to sleep. As I was coming out of anesthesia, the nurse was saying, "Kathy, you have a beautiful baby boy!"

I kept asking the nurse, "Is my baby's head normal?"

She reassured me, saying, "Yes, Kathy, it is normal." Disoriented from the effects of the anesthesia, I couldn't quite grasp the nurse's reassurance.

My thoughts were still pondering. I was trying to imagine a healthy baby. I didn't want to go through another loss.

Lying in the hospital bed, I couldn't focus on reality. Aaron brought the baby over and laid him in my arms. I knew I was truly blessed. I had a beautiful baby boy. God gave me peace in the midst of a huge blessing. I laid my head back against the pillows and shut my eyes, too happy for words.

That evening our children came to visit. Larissa and Jaron were excited. I could hear their chatter coming down the hall. They entered the room grinning from ear to ear.

Aaron handed the baby to Jaron. "He looks really cute," Jaron said, shrugging his shoulders.

Grandma stated to Jaron, "Josiah looks just like you did as a baby." After Jaron had his turn holding the baby, Larissa wanted one.

Conversation went on around Larissa, but she did not notice. She was too busy admiring her little brother. She touched the tiny, squeezed fist. She was delighted when the baby opened and closed his fingers around hers. Larissa's eyes held a twinkle that wasn't there when Naomi was born almost two years earlier. Larissa rocked gently back and forth, back and forth, never paying attention to someone asking, "May I hold Josiah now?"

I glanced at my daughter through tears. This baby was beautiful. Love swept over me and through me. What a wonder how God works everything out! "Be still and know that I am God (Psalm 46:10). God replaced my fear with hope and love.

# reminiscence

TIME MOVES ON. I FELT GOD PROMPTING me to finish my book about Naomi. *How, Lord? I don't know where to start.*

I push the whispered voice aside all spring and summer. The leaves are now turning orange and brown as fall is returning once again. I'm sitting at my kitchen table typing while I hear the baby chattering in the background.

I had a busy morning—getting the lunches packed, breakfast tackled and getting the school children off. While Josiah is napping, I manage to prop my legs up in the recliner chair and take time to read the Bible. It's the nudge I need to try and finish my story. I sensed that the Lord was leading me to focus my attention on the final part. As God worked in my heart, I welcomed the thought to reminisce. I think God is showing me there is more to tell.

Once again, a reminder. Every time I walk to the car

from the church house and see a gray, marble, heart-shaped marker or see the hospital as we drive by, I remember. *Why don't memories just evaporate?* I wonder. They can't, because memories are a part of who we are. They are a part of life. We can't wear them out like a pair of shoes, then discard them in the nearest trash can.

Ponder a Bible verse. "My thoughts are not your thoughts, neither are your ways my ways" (Isaiah 55:8).

It's been two and one half years since our loss. I especially feel the sense of our daughter's loss when her birthday comes around.

I am able to share the loss of our precious little girl with others who have felt the sting of death. It feels like something is changing inside when I share my experience.

I feel like a new, velvety red rose pushing up through the hard, cold ground on a bright, cool spring morning. The sun glistens on my soft red petals as I can vividly see the beginning of a new bloom ready to unfold all its glorious beauty.

When others have felt alone and scared, I have shared their pain and sorrow. I was once in a tunnel so dark that I thought there would never be light again.

I remind myself—you can see in the dark with God's help.

When I heard of someone who had lost a jewel, it gave me the opportunity to reach out to them and pray for them. Each time I grew. *Lord, you knew everything would work out as planned.* "And we know that all things work together for good to them that love God, to them who are called according to his purpose" (Romans 8:28).

*Naomi was not a mistake or a passing of judgment.* My thoughts repeated this over and over after her death. She was my opportunity to grow and to let my heart become teachable.

My path continues. I still cry at times and get weary. Time has passed, but at times it seems like it happened just yesterday. I still miss Naomi, but I know she's safe with Jesus. My heart still longs to hold her. Beauty is the making of a rose, but there has to be pruning, which is painful.

# comfort and peace

EVERY CHILD THAT GOD CREATES IS SPECIAL.
I learned that you cannot replace one baby with another.
"For thou hast possessed my reins: thou hast covered me
in my mother's womb. I will praise thee; for I am fearfully
and wonderfully made: marvelous are thy works; and that
my soul knoweth right well. My substance was not hid from
thee, when I was made in secret, and curiously wrought in
the lowest parts of the earth. Thine eyes did see my substance,
yet being unperfect; and in thy book all my members were
written, which in continuance were fashioned, when as yet
there was none of them." (Psalm 139:13-16). These verses say
that God created life in the womb and He knows us.

My feelings were in a turmoil as I asked questions. *How
can I go on without my baby? Why me when everyone else has
more children than I do?* "And the peace of God, which passeth
all understanding, shall keep your hearts and minds through

Christ Jesus" (Philippians 4:7). I often repeated this verse over and over. It would give me peace and I felt God was guarding my heart.

"Be strong and of a good courage, fear not, nor be afraid of them: for the Lord thy God, he it is that doth go with thee; he will not fail thee, nor forsake thee" (Deuteronomy 31:6). God never left me even though I thought He did. God is the only one that can truly comfort and heal us. Through all circumstances God will walk with us.

I communicated my feelings to my husband and my close friend. It was a great comfort in knowing that someone else was there to support me.

At times I felt as if I were the only one who ever walked through a tunnel so dark you couldn't find your way out. I longed to find someone who went through a tunnel like I did.

During the darkest moments I wondered, *Where is God?* Now I wonder why I asked these questions? I found through reading God's Word that God never left me. He carried me through the most devastating time of my life. As I cried and prayed in my heart to God, I began to truly experience comfort.

God was with Aaron and me as we told our children. He was there that morning I left the hospital with empty arms and a broken heart.

He gives me peace and understanding in the midst of my loss so that I can share and help other women through their loss.

God created life with a purpose. I feel God created Naomi for a special reason. When I face Naomi's birth date, grief settles once again in my heart. Experiencing these feelings over every year is a healthy way to ease my pain.

I look back at all the blessings Naomi's life has been to me and my family.

God worked in my life, making it more stable.

My marriage is stronger.

I count my children as a blessing.

I am able to deeply share with others who have lost a little one.

My moments of grief had a purpose that I didn't realize till today as I write from my heart. God's timing and handiwork had its place and moment in my life when I thought life wasn't fair.

I couldn't see at the time of my loss what God was trying to do for me. His grace and mercy has amazed me.

The challenges and difficulties of losing Naomi gave me two choices:

Grow through this experience and help others, or become a hard, bitter woman who God couldn't use for His honor and glory.

Naomi colors the way I look at responses towards my other children. I am more vulnerable over their welfare. I overreact when Josiah falls or bumps his head.

I could have lost more. My peace with God was one. I am more stable with God as my firm foundation. He has never left me to walk alone.

Naomi was one of the most positive experiences of my life. Positive because of what God did in my heart, what He taught me and the way He used other people to touch my life.

Grief still strikes me occasionally. It's then that I go back to the arms of God.

Children are God's painting of bright, colorful innocence. Mothers wipe noses, kiss little owies and lovingly hold their children and read to them. Taking a little one's warm hand will lead you and me down a path of life filled with love.

# letting go and letting God

THE TITLE FOR THIS CHAPTER WAS DIFFICULT because letting Naomi rest with Jesus is hard. It didn't mean that I had to forget her. Letting go allowed my heart to heal.

I learned and discovered from reading God's Word that the greatest joy in having a child is to be able to give our children freely back to God.

We mothers all have to prepare to let go of our precious children. It causes pain. Yes, but it's a healthy process that we go through. I discovered this by watching my mother-in-law. She reared ten children. Eight are gone from home and married. The relationships I have observed are bound in her heart.

As a closing to my story of grief and the wonderful things God did for us, I want to share one final story. I'm amazed that God still uses angels to help us through difficult times.

I was very sick and Aaron took me to the emergency room when I was five months pregnant with Naomi. The lights were bright in the emergency room. I felt miserable. I couldn't breathe, and I felt like a pincushion. The nurses tried to get an I.V. going but to no avail. They blew four veins. The doctor came through the door hurriedly and said, "We are going to have to prep you for surgery to put in a central I.V. line."

I was very afraid. I took a deep breath and scanned the room for Aaron. His eyes held a tender mercy. His smile tightened with a grim look. We silently prayed that God would send someone that could get an I.V. going without having to have a central line.

In walked a male nurse wearing a big smile. He said, "I am here to start your I.V."

I responded, "What is your name?"

He looks at me and says, "My name is Mud."

Aaron looks at him, asking, "Are you sure you can get the I.V. in?"

Mud states, "Yes, I can."

I look at the nurse with apprehension. Mud says, "Don't worry."

I held out my hand and let him try to put in an I.V. Mud got the I.V. in with no problem. I smiled and said, "Thank you."

He said, "Good-bye."

Later that evening we asked a different nurse, "Can you get Mud so we can thank him?"

"Who?" asked the nurse.

"Mud, the one who came in and got my I.V. going."

The nurse looked puzzled. "There is no one here by that

name."

Aaron and I look at each other with understanding and amazement. Aaron said, "God sent an angel to help you."

It was an amazing feeling to know that God was looking out for me even then. With tears of gratitude, I rejoiced at how God showed His loving-kindness.

# *mothers of faith*

HANNAH WAS A MOTHER WHO PRAYED diligently for a baby. I learned from reading her story that she grieved too. She experienced the pain of letting go.

Hannah also got discouraged when she couldn't bear any children, but she remained faithful to God.

Prayer opens up an avenue for God to work in our lives. Hannah discovered as it says in 1 Samuel 1:19, 20 that prayer and faith in God is effective.

Hannah's discouragement can be easily understood. "And she was in bitterness of soul, and prayed unto the Lord, and wept sore" (1 Samuel 1:10).

Hannah poured out her heart's desire to God. Could Hannah surrender and fulfill her promise to God? Yes, because she became broken before God. She surrendered herself into a humble servant for Him. Hannah rejoiced in submission. She sang praises to God in her heart. "And Hannah prayed, and said, My heart rejoices in the Lord, mine horn is exalted in the Lord: my mouth is enlarged over mine enemies; because I rejoice in thy salvation. There is none holy as the Lord: for there is none beside thee: neither is there any rock like our God" (1 Samuel 2:1,2).

"Delight thyself also in the Lord: and he shall give thee the desires of thine heart" (Psalm 37:4). This verse is a promise that God made to us. God will not always answer our prayers in the way we want Him to. He will fulfill the desires of our hearts as He sees best. I can relate to this, because I desperately wanted Him to heal Naomi. God knew, and saw what was best for my life. I can see now that losing Naomi was what I needed to bring me closer to Him.

Hannah was distressed over being childless. Elkanah's second wife Peninnah ridiculed Hannah. "And her adversary also provoked her sore, for to make her fret, because the Lord had shut up her womb" (1 Samuel 1:6). I fretted over not having another child for nearly eight years. It was extremely difficult to see family members and friends with little bundles to love and cherish. I committed my life to the Lord by entrusting everything to Him, including my children and my husband.

I, too, longed for more children. After eight years, we had Naomi. What delight! Then suddenly she left.

Discouragement caused my life to become bitter at the time of my loss. I didn't want to eat. I wasn't motivated to do anything except sit and watch the world go by. I allowed self-pity to take over.

Even though Hannah had discouragement, she remained faithful to God. She prayed on a daily basis. "And they rose up in the morning early, and worshipped before the Lord" (1 Samuel 1:19a). Hannah's discouragement was lifted. Her face showed it. "And her countenance was no more sad" (1 Samuel 1:18b).

Through the journey of Hannah's life I have learned to remain faithful in difficult times. It isn't easy.

"And she said, O my lord, as thy soul liveth, my lord, I am the woman that stood by thee here, praying unto the Lord. For this child I prayed, and the Lord hath given me my petition which I asked of him. Therefore have I lent him to the Lord; as long as he liveth he shall be lent to the Lord" (1 Samuel 1:26-28a).

Hannah gave up what she longed for—her son. She dedicated her entire life to God. She committed God to control her son's life. I can truly say that today I am glad I gave Naomi back to God. Naomi doesn't have to experience pain, suffering or loss. She is experiencing pure happiness and utter bliss. She is also with her brother or sister.

Yes, I still long for her at times. But one day, I know I will meet her once again.

Sarah was also a faithful mother. "Through faith also Sara herself received strength to conceive seed, and was delivered of a child when she was past age, because she judged him faithful who had promised" (Hebrews 11:11).

Sarah did not always surrender easily. She was also tempted to control circumstances around her. When God's promise of a baby didn't come right away, Sarah decided to control the situation herself.

This shows a lack of faith on Sarah's part. Her plans brought rejection of Ishmael and anger. Sarah grew in faith and truly surrendered her heart to God. Was it easy for Sarah to submit in meekness and a quiet spirit?

Why did she doubt that God would give her a child? "Now Abraham and Sarah were old and well stricken in age; and it ceased to be with Sarah after the manner of women" (Genesis 18:11). Sarah thought she was too old to bear children. She knew that she couldn't, because her child-bearing years were over. Sarah gave herself over to God's will. She became a mother of many nations.

The blessings that God gives us outweigh what we give up. I gave up Naomi and received many blessings.

My life is in order with God's Word.

Being able to help a friend through a loss.

Building bridges of friendships.

Another baby. A little boy named Josiah.

Tiny Hands
*if you're grieving*

MEMORIAL IDEAS

Make a scrapbook of your baby. Use photos, lock of hair, poems, stickers, birth certificate, death certificate. Include your other children.

Using mini poems make a small scrapbook for someone else who lost a baby.

Scrapbook Ministries, Ronald and Sherri Rohrer, 147 North Shirk Road, New Holland, PA 17557.

Meet with someone you trust to express yourself.

*Threads of Hope, Pieces of Joy* is a good resource Bible study to do with a friend. Their address is: Loving and Caring, 1905 Olde Homestead Lane, Lancaster, PA 17601.

Make a collage by using photographs and a favorite poem. Frame the collage and hang it somewhere in your house.

Have your children make their own little scrapbook using stickers, poems, photos and footprints and handprints.

Put your poem along with your baby's birth date in the newspaper.

Save your baby's clothing that he/she wore. Make a special box for them by using a plastic container and adding baby stickers to the outside of the container.

Put your favorite poem on a doily and hang it up.

# Tiny Hands
## *books to help you*

*A Time to Be Borne* Comfort for mothers of miscarried babies, Carlisle Press, 1.800.852.4482.

*Free to Grieve* Maureen Rank, Bethany House Publishing, 1998.

*Empty Arms: Coping with Miscarriage, Stillbirth and Infant Death* Sherokee Ilse, Wintergreen Press, 1982, 1990, 2002.

*A Rose in Heaven* Dawn Siegrist, Waltman, Paradise Publications, 1999.

*Threads of Hope, Pieces of Joy* Teale Fackler and Gwen Kik, Benjamin Books, 1999.

*In Memory of Michael* Wanda M. Yoder, Christian Light Publications, Inc. 1998.

*A Tear In My Heart* 29 stories of woman with tubal pregnancies, complied by Elva Shirk, Carlisle Press, 1.800.852.4482

# Tiny Hands
## *resources for support*

Share—Pregnancy and Infant Loss Support, Inc. is to serve those whose lives are touched by the tragic death of a baby through early pregnancy loss, stillbirth or in the first few months of life.

National Share Office, St. Joseph Health Center, 300 First Capital Drive, St. Charles, MO 63301. Office: 636.947.6164, toll-free: 800.821.6819.

*Broken Hearts, Living Hope* is a free newsletter for families who have lost children of any age. Carol A. Raney, Ed., 11040 SW Gaarde St. #8, Tigard, OR 97224-3736.

# Anencephaly

## Normal Infant

## Anencephalic Infant

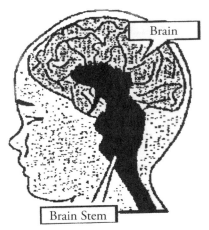

Brain

Brain Stem

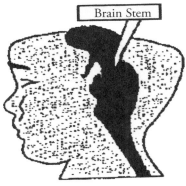

Brain Stem